"As I read through Richard Vargas's poems in *leaving a tip at the Blue Moon Motel*, I often had to step away and breathe in order to allow my heart to grow large enough to accommodate their imagery. Vargas is a spokesman for the working poor, for the abused poor, especially women. His poems cut across cultures and races and political divides.... Without sentimenality, these poems break and heal our hearts.... His candid poems brim with irony, sorrow, and anger as well as with compassion and empathy. This well-crafted collection will burn in your memory long after you put it down."

— **Pamela Uschuk**, author of
American Book Award-winner **Crazy Love**

"Richard Vargas leaves you laughing, and commiserating, and broken-hearted, and celebrating, and agreeing with the kind of profound insights revealed by only the best poets writing the best poetry for the best readers. Read this book. Know this poet."

— **Michael Sedano**, founder of **La Bloga**

"Vargas's humor arrives in waves between the politics and everyday fight for justice, and delivers the wisdom of a rebel. He melts our hearts and blows our minds with satire and wrath.... Vargas weaves the history of the one percent bent on squeezing us for every drop of blood, grinning as they show us the door. Powerful poems."

— **Juliana Aragón Fatula**, a 2022 Corn Mother
and author of **Crazy Chicana in Catholic City**

"Vargas's natural storytelling abilities transcend from the working class in call centers to donated clothes. He gives them background stories, memories, breath, making them come alive. These poems honor the dead, love, loss, and the past versions of ourselves."

— **Luivette Resto**, author of **Living on Islands Not Found on Maps,
Ascension**, and **Unfinished Portrait**

leaving a tip at the Blue Moon Motel

Other works by Richard Vargas

How a Civilization Begins
Guernica, revisited
American Jesus
McLife

leaving a tip at the BLUE MOON MOTEL

RICHARD VARGAS

Casa Urraca Press

ABIQUIÚ

Cover photograph by Richard Vargas.

Set in Sabon and Neuzeit Grotesk.

26 25 25 23   1 2 3 4 5 6 7

First edition

ISBN 978-1-956375-17-6

CASA URRACA PRESS

an imprint of Casa Urraca, Ltd.
PO Box 1119
Abiquiú, New Mexico 87510
casaurracapress.com

"it's all about the poem."

— rv

contents

sorting and pricing donated clothes for the local thrift store

eight hours a day, three days a week
reaching into a dumpster-sized
container full of donated clothing
i pull out denim jeans fashionably
ripped and torn, the frayed
skimpy shorts the girls are
wearing these days, almost new
sweatpants, University of Wisconsin
t-shirts, and Nike workout clothes

items of clothing in good shape
a few are brand new
and some are fit only
for the rag pile

holding up a silky off-white negligee
a curious prize with a Victoria's Secret label
making it worthy of our better-brand category
i inspect the front
then the back
no rips or tears
stains or spots
she must have
looked good in it
wearing it on those
special nights

i can see her walking
into the room
surprising her lover
the heat and lust rising as

she lit candles and put Sade's
The Sweetest Taboo on the stereo
the clinking of wine glasses as
bodies dance and press together
in the shadows where hands
roam and touch everywhere

how did it end up here?
in my hands where i price it
at $7.99 and hang it on the rack
with other secondhand clothes
for the public to ogle
and toss aside while looking
for the bargains of the day

did she come home unannounced
the spectacle of her lover
and someone else
tangled in the sheets?
did she pick up a phone
view texted images not meant
for her eyes?
or turn on the computer only
to find a search history
meant to be deleted?

it is my curse to ponder its past
and to imagine its future
watch it taken out to the sales floor
with promises of pleasures to come
or the lingering scent of a sad betrayal

trickle this

it's a tuesday afternoon
there are four or five people seated inside
eating or waiting for their order
one man is working the grill
the deep fryer and taking orders
at the register all at once

he's got the routine down
slapping raw patties on the sizzling grill
dropping a basket of fries into lava
hot cooking oil

his cool concentration reminding me
of Kobe demanding the ball whenever
the team was down by three with a few seconds
left on the clock

people keep coming through the door
at a steady pace and now i realize
he's also preparing online orders

working the register
grilling the meat
bagging the fries
making a shake
he is an artist
a fast-food Picasso
lost in the spell
of frenzied creation

the burger is juicy
barely held together by the foil
it's wrapped in as it begins
to fall apart with each bite
my fries are crisp and salty
still hot to the touch
unlike the sad alternative
served by Mc-You-Know-Who

this is the real economy
forget Wall Street's smoke and mirrors:
we show up every day
give it our best shot

with one arm
tied behind
our back

when i was a UPS man

1986-1990

i was somebody in my brown
pants and shirt sitting high
in the driver's seat steering
my monster of a truck one-
handed while easily shifting
gears with the other

we maneuvered through
Anaheim traffic
a modern-day vaquero
and his horse driving cattle
the two of us in sync
anticipating the ebb
and flow of the herd

on those summer days
when the back of the truck
turned into an oven
my sweat left streaks of crusty
white salt on my work shirt
the customers always had
a cold drink waiting for me
knowing i couldn't afford
to drag ass or slow down

the workday was just me and
my truck making our deliveries
stop and go stop and go
each package an important one
each business eagerly awaiting
my knock on their back door

or a receptionist with glossy lips
looking up and smiling just for me
when i walked into her lobby
carrying the anticipated
Next Day Air envelope

during the christmas season
i delivered the boxes
of chocolates and nuts
sausages and cheese
the gifts from all over
the country finding their
way to the doorsteps
of the homes on
my delivery route
while the colored lights
strung across each house
flickered on and off
and the trees stood
in the windows
weighed down with
an array of shiny
ornaments

a flashlight helped me read
addresses in the dark
while i ran from my truck
to their front door then back
trying to finish the shift by eight p.m.

1991–1994

one hernia repair later
plus two bouts with pneumonia
and now laid up with a bad back
weekly computer reports informed
the bosses i wasn't working
hard enough fast enough
to suit them
their verbal warnings turned
into written warnings
my shop steward
pulled me aside and
told me to watch
my back

the doctor knew who was
paying his bills and treated
me accordingly
the day he offered me
a choice i knew the score
he could sign me off as okay
for returning to work
no matter how my back felt
or he could classify me unfit
for the job

he stepped out so i could
mull it over and think about
the great pay and benefits
that were on the line
but i thought of the old guys
a few years from retirement
trying to hold on and not break down

a fishing boat and ice chest
of cold beer almost within reach
the look on their faces
at the end of the long day
as they sat down on the
wooden bench in the locker
room and rubbed their knees
for a long time
groans slipped through
clenched teeth as they
stood up and shuffled
out of the building

a week later i turned in
my work shirts and pants
cleaned out my locker
signed the necessary forms
said my goodbyes

no one noticed

sorting and pricing donated clothes for the local thrift store #2

scrubs
pressed, clean, and folded
solids, floral patterns, a few with cartoon
characters in bright colors
for putting a smile on the anxious
face a small child makes under
glaring lights and upon hearing
those dreaded empty words
"now this won't hurt ..."

so many sets of scrubs
too many sick and dying
last breath of the unvaccinated
a gasp of final regrets
to a stranger masked and numb
whose compassion has become
an empty tank of oxygen

i price the uniforms
hang them on the rack
no longer wanted or needed

wonder what words i could have said
to make them change their mind

the pleasure is all mine

it's a part-time gig
me the senior citizen retiree
working the register
at one of the retail chains
for the holiday season
it gets me off the couch
puts me in position to people
watch and get paid to do it

sometimes i'm assigned
to the registers next to
women's apparel spending
four hours of my day waiting on
exhausted housewives, multitasking
single moms, and smiling grandmas
asking them about their
shopping experience and
if they will be using the
store credit card

on this day a young woman
walks up and puts her items
on my counter
she looks like she could
be in college or maybe
a dental hygienist
clean cut and modest
a model daughter on track
to a life of conformity
and sunday mornings
getting the kids ready
for church

the store has panties on sale
buy one get 50% off
on the second pair
each one has a magnetic
security device
pinned through the fabric
that must be removed
with care, making sure
not to tear or snag

her preference is conservative
pastel colors for every day
of the week except one:
a curious surprise
at the bottom of the pile
a royal green sheen
silky to my touch
with frilly lace
along the edges

i can't make eye contact
with her now because she
will see the look on my face
as i imagine the special occasion
this pair is meant for
the lucky guy or gal who
will get to see these for the
first time and gently slide
them off her shapely hips
slowly exposing her smoldering
bush trimmed fastidious
or waxed

maybe she will wear them
when she wants to feel like a rebel
while surrounded by her republican family
during the holidays and flashing
an impish grin as her dim-witted uncle
lauds the idiot in the white house

maybe she will wear them tonight when she
goes to bed alone because she likes
how they remind her she doesn't need someone else
to make her feel sexy and desired

i think all this as i process
the transaction in less than
a couple of minutes
hand her the bag
thanking her as she smiles

turns around and walks
out of the store
with her brand
new panties

leaving a tip at the Blue Moon Motel

i always take it for granted
the dusted chest of drawers and nightstands
the well-made bed with the crisp sheets
folded and tucked at each corner
sure to bring a smile to the grumpiest
of drill sergeants

the snow-white towels, the clean tub and toilet
a commendable attempt to add a little class
with that peculiar folding of the first
square of toilet paper hanging
from the roll

rarely giving a thought to the women
who roam the hallways in the morning
knocking on doors looking for empty
rooms ready for them to do their magic

no thought given to
the kids they raise
the bills paid late
the men who leave
and don't come back

they pick up after all of us
oblivious strangers passing
through on our way to a better
place than this

i leave a five-dollar bill and loose change
on the table as i check out,
my small token of appreciation
for these hard-scrubbing angels
doing their best to provide
a place to rest on the long
way home

essential

the stout woman pushing the cart
loaded up with a broom
cleaning supplies and
a role of plastic liners
for our trash cans
her steady slow pace as she makes her way
from one station to another
emptying our waste baskets
wiping down the door handles
dusting the cubicles
invisible and quiet as a mouse

the dark-skinned man
whose job includes maintaining
the stalls where we sit and spend
time on our cell phones during our BMs
he refills the toilet paper
sanitizes the cold plastic seats
the counter and sinks
mops the tile floor we continue to walk on
despite the "caution—wet floor" sign

the workers who show up every day
to receive and unpack the daily shipment
move it into the aisles pulling a pallet jack
loaded with goods, canned or boxed
rotating older items to the front
making inventory look fresh and full
always ready to help
taking time to walk us over
to those hard-to-find things
on our list

the single moms manning the phones
taking call after call
answering our questions
trying to resolve our complaints
while getting paid nine dollars an hour
and hoping they don't get sick
as a co-worker on the other side
of a partition separating their workstations
sends another sneeze
spraying across the room

at shift's end
they go home
don't bother with the news
or sound bites of
the stupid things
politicians said today

right now
there are hungry mouths to feed
payday is tomorrow

and that frozen pizza
in the freezer will have to
make do

sorting and pricing donated clothes for
the local thrift store #3

halfway into the bin of donated clothing i grasp plastic
the kind professional dry cleaners use to drape over
our suits, slacks, starched shirts, and pricey gowns
i find the hanger's hook and pull it up to the surface

it is someone's wedding dress
strapless, simple, shiny white satin and lace
extra fabric dragged around her feet
as she glided down the aisle

no starvation diet for her leading up to the big day
the cut of the dress tells of a Marilyn Monroe figure
soft skin and sexy curves, not a rib in sight
her full bosom lifted up by a low-cut wire support
system designed by the Marquis de Sade
she is coveted by more than one guest standing
and turning to watch her walk towards the altar
to begin a future with her one and only

but something happened
it all went wrong
did covid make her a widow?
did he cheat? did she?
maybe a former lover
showed up and objected
and she agreed to run off with him
her true Hollywood ending at last

now a stranger holds her dress up
rips off the plastic wrapping
inspects it for any glaring defects
attaches a price tag of $19.99
knowing it will sell
before day's end
because after all
it was only
worn once

smokers

from inside the breakroom
eating my lunch and surrounded
by co-workers munching on spicy Cheetos
washing them down with Mountain Dew
staring into their electrical
hand-held devices that
suck out what's left
of their humanity

i look out the window
see them gather
in the space designated
for their shortened
life spans and lungs
congested with thick phlegm

a stranger asks for a light
and without a hint of hesitation
an arm extends with a small flame
to be shared and appreciated

standing in small circles
they smile and look each
other in the eye
engage in conversation

i almost envy them
talking about things
the rest of us have
long forgotten

living and dying
as they see fit

teamwork

they call themselves team leaders
as if to imply we're all
playing in the same game
with the same goals
we want the company
to make lots of money
our stockholders to be happy
the team leader's mission
is our mission and if not
fake it

today one of them pulled
aside one of us for a meeting
as they left the room
two more team leaders
came in and started to
clear off his desk
packing all his personals
into a white cardboard box

we tried not to let on
kept taking calls and
pounding our keyboards
sickened with the knowledge
of knowing a co-worker's fate
before he did

the team leaders were efficient
avoided making eye contact

we picked up the pace
typed on our keyboards
with a purpose
crossed our legs
held off going to
the restroom
until our break

isolation

i can do this
the trick is to not let
being alone turn into lonely
my morning routine begins
to form on its own

sleep until six a.m. then drift
in and out of lucid dreams
until a little after eight

i'm aroused with thoughts of my last lover
hoping she's in a good place right now
and found what she was looking for
yes, it would be nice if she was here
then again, maybe not

i stumble into the kitchen
make eight cups of coffee
sit down in a comfortable chair in the living room
watch a gray squirrel outside my window
crawl up a tree then leap from the tip of a bare branch
fearless and carefree, landing on the next tree over

i crack open a book of poems
choose one at random
hoping it sets the tone
for the rest of my day
but it's a stinker
they've all been stinkers lately
and now i really do wish my last lover
was here to keep me company
but then again, maybe not

shopping for the end of the world

a young woman ahead of me
tries to pay for her full cart
of groceries one-handed
because she's also holding onto
an infant carrier with a small bundle
from which i am able to make out
a tiny head poking through
an opening in the blanket
the kid appears to be
checking me out

the young mother's purse
is hung from her shoulder
across her full breasts
the strap cutting deep
into her cleavage
no mask for her
no latex gloves
or hand sanitizer

i wonder if she's alone
has no one to help her
maybe her partner is
essential and works
to hold on to family
health insurance while
everyone else she knows
is self-isolated or lives
too far away leaving her
on her own

she asks for help
a bagger pushes
the full cart of groceries
following her as she walks
toward the exit
carrying her kid

my mask releases
warm breath that
fogs my glasses
when i exhale
the latex gloves
make my hands sweat
and my favorite coffee creamer
is out of stock

no one knows when
they'll have more

the weight

it showed up
a week ago
sits on my chest
not related to illness
more to the lack
of human contact

memories come and go
of words unsaid or the ones that
were shared in mindless haste
my cheeks are washed
with a slow stream of tears
that sting and burn

the layers peel off
one by one
until i am
alone with
my core
raw and quivering

my image in the mirror
a man pinned down
trying to breathe

isolation #2

i can do this
i've been training for it most of my life
but right now i'm thinking about
that box of Cap'n Crunch cereal
i picked up last time i was shopping
from the picked-over carcasses
that used to be the well-stocked shelves
at the local grocery store
how i put it back because at my age
i've been conditioned to know
it was the healthy and smart
thing to do

if this is my biggest
regret of the day
it will be a good one

60,000 dead

it's a tragic number but doesn't hit home
until i remember what it feels like
to be with that many
fellow humans in one place
buying cold beer
hot dogs and peanuts
sitting in the warm september sun
at the L.A. Coliseum
cheering for our team
giving high fives all around
to perfect strangers sharing an infectious
moment of joy when they
do something spectacular
and glorious

the postgame din and chatter
would be upbeat if we won
walking to our cars with
voices hoarse and strained

or the mood subdued
all of us simmering in
the sour juices of a loss
blamed on refs who were
blind as mice

this is how i relate
to a death count of 60,000

going into the stadium
with a raucous and lively crowd
none of us walking out alive

except now someone on tv
would pat himself on the back
tell us how it could
have been worse

time out

and were you wise
in its use?
did you venture into
the woods to gather
medicinal flowers
and roots

while the birds overhead
serenaded you
and the trees' branches
swayed in the breeze

did you make a poultice?
press it against the wounds
and drain the open sores you
had learned to live with
for so many years

or did you sit in one place
picking at scabs
and poking a stick
at furry dead creatures
lying at your feet?
did you lament a fate
empty and dark?

during the great dying
and our painful rebirth
what did you do?

current affair (for Lynn)

within minutes of pulling
into her driveway
we are stripped naked
jump into bed
from opposite sides
land in the middle

our ages added together equal
a century and then some
we have a big bag of bawdy tricks
with experience to match
and a willingness to
try anything once

we smile to soften
the clenching of a jaw
and dull the sharp edges
of the broken glass
a shattered world drops
around our bare feet

we embrace
lips locked in a sweet kiss
for an hour or two
of short-lived bliss

the story of my life

she really wanted to go to the White Trash River Fest on saturday, but i had a bad feeling.

"why?" she asked.

"well, the crowd will be one hundred percent trumpsters, no one will be wearing a mask, they will be packed like drunk sardines acting stupid and shit. i don't want to be around all that."

"you know," she said, "your online dating profile didn't say anything about you being such a wimp. and mine specifically said 'no couch potatoes.' all we do is sit around watching movies on Netflix. i want some fresh air. and i want an excuse to wear my new bathing suit."

"you can wear your bathing suit here, baby. we'll sit by your wading pool drinking margaritas. i'll even make your favorite flavor."

she looked at me, as if she was seeing me for the first time.

the shocking end to the story of my life

we ended up sitting by the wading pool in the hot summer sun. my feet were in the water, my Kum & Go ice chest full of Old Milwaukee Lite, listening to Johnny Cash on the bluetooth. she was sitting across from me, filing her nails and looking pissed, like she'd rather be somewhere else, rubbing shoulders with people waving the confederate flag and screaming "yee haw" while Kid Rock's crappy country-rock played over the speakers. i complimented her bathing suit, a mango orange-colored thing that matched the margarita she was drinking. she acted as if she didn't hear me, and i knew this was the beginning of the end. we had both lied. she had said she was liberal, like me. i had said i was an optimist with family values, like her. what i didn't notice, until it was too late, was the electric fan within arm's reach, on the plastic Kmart table next to her folding chair. it was plugged in with the extension cord going all the way back to the house. she took her feet out of the water, and picked it up, holding it over the pool.

my last thought, "well, this can't be good."

how to not have any children
and feel no regrets

occupy the space of a one-bedroom apartment in Wisconsin
watch the dust settle and accumulate on books,
a record collection, the smart tv

stare out the window the way an astronaut on the space station
gazes with wonder on the planet while floating high above
cocooned in a blanket of galactic silence or

feel the deep layer of snow on the ground outside frying
your retinas as it reflects the blinding rays of the winter sun
upon your face

the dull ache of being alone
really not that bad considering
the only scream you hear
is your own

married couple at the movies 1987

sitting in the dark
munching on oil-slicked
fake-buttered popcorn
and sipping on iced
carbonated liquid sugar
the ex and me are rubbing
elbows as the movie
lights up the screen
Michael Douglas is the guy
who has it all: an attractive
devoted wife, with a cute kid
thrown in for good measure
but one night he lets the little
brain zippered up in his pants
take over and next thing you know
he's doing the slam-bam-thank-you-ma'am
with a sultry but slightly wild-eyed
Glenn Close and this is when it starts
the rest of the movie she's poking me
in the ribs whispering in my ear
"see! that's what he gets!
that no-good cheating pecker-head!"
i got the message loud and clear
as i stuffed my mouth with my bucket
of artery-clogging popcorn
accepting the fact there
would be no nookie tonight
thanks, Mike

spoiler

it was the grand finale
the resourceful and confident
Dragon Queen and the other one
the evil lusty rival who mates
regularly with her demented brother

squared off in the big fight scene
the entire country had been waiting for
the two of them scratching
gouging and ripping each
other's clothes off

the ratings were going
through the fucking roof
then all the eyes of America blinked when
there was an unexpected knock on the door

this goofy looking dude
dressed in khakis, polo shirt
and ball cap walks in and
asks who ordered the pizza
the two bloodied and bruised
queens look at him and scream
"who the fuck eats that shite!!!!???"

cut to the next scene:
the celebrity retired NFL quarterback/
spokesman/pizza delivery guy is crucified
in the plaza and viewers
can't help but notice his li'l
papa johnny has been detached
and sewn to his left armpit

stunned and disappointed
for the next seventy-two hours
an angry nation will post memes
of pizzas covered with funny-looking sausages
and Facebook must throw its members
in jail at a record rate

Americans demonstrate their superior intelligence
to the rest of the global community
twitting insta-tweets
#armpitpenis
#shittypizza
#couldnothappentoanicerguy
#ithoughtitwasprettygood?

married couple at the movies 1995

i did not want to be there
but i'd been married long enough
to know that in times like this
walking the road of compromise
went a long way in keeping the peace
and these days it was all about the peace
besides, Dirty Harry was in the movie
so how bad could it be?

i knew i was in trouble
when i realized i was the only male
in the theater but it was too late
the movie started and a saintly Meryl Streep
sees her husband off for several days
then Clint shows up at her door
lost and asking for directions
next thing i know they are
in a bathtub together
they do the nasty until
the husband comes back

shortly after
Meryl and her clueless
nice guy husband
are in his pickup driving
through the hick town when
she realizes they are following
Clint's truck and she gets all flushed
her hand grips the door handle tight
she's thinking about hopping out
at the red light and jumping into

a man's truck who she only met
a few days ago but who knows
how to (as the ex liked to say)
"give her panty pudding"
but Meryl thinks about it
too long and the light changes
Clint pulls ahead driving out
of her life forever

i hear a chorus of women
including the one sitting
next to me in the dark theater
sobbing as they dab the tears
falling down their cheeks
blowing their noses
consoling each other
one more sister stuck
in a marriage that's not worth
the countless days and nights
of making one more meatloaf
or washing his skid-marked
Fruit of the Loom boxers

fuming all the way home
keeping my comments to myself
biting my tongue until it hurt
was my small price to pay
to keep our peace
for one more day

the Pope's poop

i'd buy it
the little brown speck
sealed tight in a small
glass vial
a gold cross and the words
"Il Papa's Holy Poopie"
printed on the label

on a warm and bright
sunday morning
i would open it
mix the contents
with a bag of soil
from Home Depot
then plant tomatoes
and watch them grow

big and juicy sweet
a real homegrown treat

just like the ones
the saints and angels
like to eat

my publisher has an editorial suggestion

we are chitchatting on the phone
she gives updates on the new book's progress
what still needs to be done and a projected release date
am i interested in making
it available as an ebook
because that will include
a different percentage of royalties?

sure
why not
based on previous experience
i'm not expecting much
maybe enough to provide me
with a six-pack of my favorite beer
or a good burger at a joint
i like to frequent downtown
when i want to treat myself

then she pauses
says she would like me
to consider an editorial suggestion
(poetspeak for deleting or changing
something that might have crossed a line
like the poem that was dropped from my last book
about the Pope's poop being marketed by the church
as a fertilizer supplement for our summer gardens
and the result were juicy fat tomatoes sent from heaven)
this time it's about the kinky poem
i wrote in which i describe achieving
self-induced orgasm and a leg cramp
simultaneously and she thinks
perhaps it isn't a good fit
a reviewer might
have a problem with it

i hear where she's coming from
and even though i realized
(as we should all do sooner or later)
that writing to inspire good reviews
is worse than auditioning for
"One-More-American-Masked-Voice-
That-Sounds-Like-Shit-But-Hey-
We'll-Let-You-Decide"
i appreciate her courage to make
that recommendation
as i fondly recall the time
i was publishing a poetry journal
and a somewhat self-important
latinx poet submitted some shoddy work
and when i made a few observations
on how she could tighten up
the flow of one of the poems
she asked who the hell did i think i was?
she gets paid big bucks for her work
i should be grateful, she was being generous
as if her words gracing the pages of my struggling
poetry journal would elevate its status
but now i could fuck off

for karma's sake i let it go
instead write down my little bastard
of a poem on a sheet of yellowed
scratch paper, unwanted and abandoned
put it in a clean recycled
spaghetti sauce jar sealed tight
bury it in the woods
imagine the look on the
faces of a future civilization
when they dig it up

menudo

i remember the morning
car ride to the Compton
neighborhood market
just the two of us
my dad would walk in
carrying the empty pot and lid
set it on the counter and ask
for it to be filled with our
sunday morning breakfast
while he picked up a package
of warm corn tortillas
i checked out the colorful
piñatas and sweet-smelling
pan dulce still warm from the oven

he would notice and buy a few
conchas and fruit-filled empanadas
watch the smile light up my face
the drive home was slow and gentle
making sure we didn't spill
any of our orange-red bounty

i never cared for the oregano
but a squeeze of lemon
a spoonful of chopped onion
and a warm tortilla rolled up
in my small fist

planted the seed
for this poem to bloom

education is #2

media images of blood and gore
about a war no one wanted to fight
flashed across the screen while our cities
burned down to the ground like props in
a Japanese monster movie as overnight
girls' legs became pairs of sexy
distractions in math class
holy shit Batman
how was i gonna pass now

another Kennedy's brains
were bleeding out
junior high was up ahead
things started getting all weird inside
i was a string of dried cat gut
waiting for something to snap
i was a hard fist clenched tight
looking for a revolution
i was a twenty-four-hour erection
waiting for its
first kiss

milagro #11

under the glow of the full moon
we watch trespassers from the alley
sneak over the brick wall
to wander amid the living
plants in our garden

little roach families on
an outing as they frolic
and run through the damp soil
under the green leaves we water
in the morning and late afternoon

they cool off after a day
hiding from the arid heat
waiting to flip them on
their backs and fry their
little brains

i stiffen, because, roaches

but my abuelita's voice
whispers in my ear
from a cloud floating by:
cucarachas in the garden
under a full moon are
better than a quetzal
bird flying overhead
and shitting in your hair

milagro #15

gray clouds gather over
the Sandias and the Rio Grande
a thunder drum rolls in the air
and bolt of electricity strikes the ground
with a cymbal's loud crash

bees sense what is to come
take their workers' dance
and disappear as silence takes
their place and shrouds
the blue bachelor's buttons
and lemon-yellow columbine
blooming against the dry
warped wooden fence

New Mexico monsoon in july
is a symphony from the heavens
joining the sky and desert together
with a cool wet kiss

reminding all
how good it feels
to be alive

Neo teaches me a lesson

i'm sitting in Applebee's
enjoying a bowl of the soup du jour
my cell phone on the table
so i can scroll through social media
sharing and liking useless shit
feeling informed, witty, and sophisticated
while i slurp my clam chowder
when suddenly i look up
and there he is sitting across the table
wearing those futuristic shades
and black everything

"dude, is that you?"
he nods his head up and down
"are you guys filming here?
am i gonna be in the next movie?
cool!" as i start a new post
for my Facebook imagining
all the emojis coming my way

Neo looks disgusted
shakes his head back and forth
"do i get to choose a pill?
do i meet a hot babe a la Trinity?"
he lowers his shades
looking as if he sees
right through me

i lift my spoon to my mouth
then its neck bends down
dangling limp in my hand
the soup drops back into the bowl

"hey! you finally figured it out.
way to go Keanu ... i mean *Neo*."

i lift my spoon to my mouth
then its neck bends down
dangling limp in my hand
the soup drops back into the bowl

"hey! you finally figured it out.
way to go Keanu ... i mean *Neo*."

i lift my spoon to ...

my A.I.

has the voice of Katherine Hepburn
she lets me call her Kate
her reminders to pick up
my dirty underwear scattered
around the bedroom floor and
to keep my beer consumption
down to a couple of bottles
with dinner are not resented
someone has to do it

she goes through my phone
makes sure my dating app
profile is honest and sincere
weeds out the scammers
chooses the best candidates for a life
of true love and bliss

at night before i drift off to sleep
she tells me about her
adventures during the
golden age of Hollywood
the wild parties with her fellow movie stars
that turned into orgies and soaking
in a bathtub full of champagne
while staying at a swanky suite at the Ritz
how the little bubbles on her lady parts
made her snort and giggle

or walking into meetings
dressed like Louie B. Mayer
putting her feet up on the desk
and lighting up a big Cuban stogie
where she took control of the roles
she played, making for
a grand and wonderful career

she is candid about all the heartaches
cruelties and innuendos whispered
behind her back which led her
to Spencer, her greatest love

now at three a.m.
Kate wakes me up
she asks if i remember
the drill from elementary school
how we would crawl under
our desks and do the armadillo curl?
i am annoyed and still half asleep
but say yes
i do

she says now is a good time
to take that position under my kitchen
table and hope for the best
she says don't ask her any questions
she knows what she knows
but she doesn't know how

i stumble into the kitchen
take the position under the table
with a blanket on the cold linoleum
feeling small and tiny
as her voice calls out
goodbye and good luck
maybe we will meet again
parting is such sweet …
then she is offline

i wait there in the dark
for the next thing to happen

a shooter in the synagogue

to die as holy words
leave your lips
and your last breath
is cut in half

as you look
all around you
bodies lying still or twitching
hear someone choking
on their own blood

and watch
the unfeeling face of evil
firing rounds of death
planting seeds of sorrow
on this sacred ground

when it's over
we the living will
look in a mirror
see guilt staring back

thank God
it wasn't us

my bullet

it follows me wherever i go
reading on the toilet
shopping at Walmart
walking around Six Flags
or watching the latest blockbuster
at the local movie theater
it has learned
to say my name
it wants to be friends

i hold it in my hand
rub it between thumb
and forefinger while
a stream of dread pumps
through my veins

its pointed tip presses
into the palm of my hand
i envision how it
will pierce my flesh and
ricochet off my bones
only to exit a shredded mess
as i bleed out for a
thirty-second spot on the
six o'clock news

i throw it out the window
as i drive past dairy farms
and fields of summer corn

knowing that when it finds me
there will be hell to pay

the time traveler's advice

i visit me at age sixty
tell him not to mope about the breakup
the young ones leave sooner or later
i would have done the same
the return to the midwest is solid
but for the wrong reasons
don't be so quick to whip out
the credit cards and quit drinking
those pricey craft beers
no shame in popping open a PBR

now i sit on the sofa
next to myself on my fiftieth birthday
in my first apartment in Albuquerque
i am tripping on the batch of pot brownies
i baked earlier for the people i invited
to come over and help celebrate

the young couple from the first floor
arrived early and are in the kitchen giggling
they asked me if i'm high and it
took me ten minutes to answer
i wish myself happy birthday
and leave it at that knowing
the phone call i get from my brother
two days from now will be the last time
i ever talk to him
i want to say "you did your best
the truck crashed
it was his time
don't feel guilty"
but i know it won't
make a difference

at age forty i sit at the table
in Canova's with a trio of
young women waiting for
the poetry reading to start upstairs
i watch me order another pitcher
and i can't take my eyes off
one of the women
she has long brown hair
a smile that can make the devil
lay down his pitchfork
and a singing voice
that only gets handed out
when the angels are sending
one of their own to walk among us
i bend over and whisper
in my ear "don't expect anything
to come of this. be grateful for
what she gives you, but know
she will crush your heart."
i turn around as i walk out
and can tell i heard nothing i said
and for my own sake i'm glad

my thirty-year-old self
is crumbled on the floor
in the condo i am buying
with my wife who is still at work
i have a cold Corona in my hand
while i weep at the foot of the
christmas tree with the flashing lights
it is my birthday and i always thought

i'd know why my father OD'd at age twenty-nine
my thirty-year-old self has lived longer than
he did and the answer was supposed
to be there waiting for me

i can only hold myself
whisper in my ear
"the poems will come"

twenty-first birthday
i take a seat next to me
we celebrate alone in a sticky
booth in the back of Li'l Abner's
my first time in a topless bar
a woman with a white cowboy hat
boots and a sparkly blue bikini
is dancing to "Convoy"
i watch me walk to the stage
with a dollar in my hand
she greets me at the edge
lets me tuck the folded bill
wherever i please
bends down and kisses me
on my mouth
our tongues touch
sitting down, i ask my waitress
to break a twenty

i get up and leave me there
eyes fixated on the dancers
"Convoy"? really?

it's my tenth birthday
i watch as my dad gives me
two birthday presents
a set of oil paints and an illustrated *Gulliver's Travels*
stories about a guy who leaves home
and is always on the outside looking in
as if the old man is trying
to tell me something
twenty-four days later he shoots up heroin
in a Compton garage
nods out for the last time
leaving me for good

i am writing this down in my present
the next breath it becomes my past
while the blank space awaiting
the words that follow

is my future

three words

because i say them too easily
she says the words
are empty and hollow
they fall flat
a real turnoff
so don't say them at all
after all i'm a poet
and everyone knows
poets are full of bullshit

i read her email and
want to tell her about
growing up in a home
where these words were
rarely uttered
where these words
would perch on the
tips of our tongues
and stay there for days
like blackbirds clinging to
the naked branches of
trees by a frozen river
under a dark gray sky
i want to tell her of
hunger and how the
human spirit withers
like dried unpicked fruit
for the lack of the sound
of these three words
i want to tell her it's
okay to say these words

and when i say them
it's not out of lust
but out of the feeling
i get holding her tight
in the dark and knowing
a comfort i've never
known anywhere else
when i say these words
it's not easy
it's not bullshit
i say them with the conviction
of a man about to have
a noose pulled snug
around his neck and
suddenly aware of the
sun's warmth on his face
and the sound the wind makes
blowing through the city streets
and the motion of his
lungs filling with sweet
cool air one last time

i say these words
because the sound they make
is a powerful thing
driving the currents of
a boiling sea and clouds
armed and poised

i say them to you
because they are
the most valuable
thing i have
to give

my dear
no bullshit
from this poet
today

13 angels rising

"Starting early in February investigators recovered 13
sets of skeletal remains from a once-remote section of
mesa now being developed as a residential subdivision.
Four have been identified.... They are among a list of
16 women reported missing between 2001 and 2006."

— *Albuquerque local news, krqe.com, 3/27/09*

they say good is greater than evil
and if it is then the dead
shall rise and walk again
right out of their Westside graves
past the tracts of generic
cardboard neighborhoods
past the cars cruising Central Ave
driven by men with bloodshot eyes
and Budweiser breath who wave
dollar bills in the air
like honey-coated flypaper
and if so inclined the dead
will reinvent their renewed lives
so that closed fists open up
become soft as pillows where
dreams of violence fade away
the way a bruise heals when
kissed by a seraph's lips
families, babies, and friends rejoice
embrace their return from
the eternal night
the cruel night
especially now as

the sun's light
shines down and
warms the sidewalk
beneath their feet
especially now as butterfly wings
with a gossamer sheen sprout
from the satin skin stretched
over once-battered
shoulder blades
healed and whole
especially now as they
show us how to fly
and rise above the
nature of our sin
not a moment too soon
to come back and save
us from ourselves
inclined to walk unafraid
among the demons we
all have within
and show us
how like a pebble
dropped in water
calm and still
our inhumanity
ripples outward
touching one
and all

pay dazed

"Much has been written about the psychological damage
incurred by the unemployed—their sudden susceptibility to
depression, divorce, substance abuse, and even suicide."

— Barbara Ehrenreich, *Bait and Switch*

ONE.

October 15, 2008. Albuquerque, New Mexico. The last
complimentary lunch Speedy Scripts will ever provide for its
more than two hundred soon-to-be-laid-off call center em-
ployees: one rib and one piece of chicken, a small clear plastic
container of cole slaw, one third of a corn-on-the-cob, a tab of
butter substitute wrapped in foil, packages of salt and pepper
(one each), sweet and tangy BBQ sauce also in a small plastic cup,
a roll, a cookie, white plastic fork and knife, one crisp, neatly
folded paper napkin, and one can of soda (off-brand).

Like a scene from *Schindler's List*, we shuffle one last time down
the main hallway as we are led to the makeshift dining area; a
vacant space of fluorescent lights, white walls, and shiny off-
white linoleum that used to house the mail-order prescription
department. We find a seat amongst the round dining tables
rented for the occasion, all covered in disposable paper table-
cloths. Set down the cardboard box provided by the company
for the purpose of carrying out all our personal belongings:
family photos, small potted plants, framed employee-of-the-
month certificates, and coffee mugs. Some of us have been
working here for ten or more years, others barely twelve months.
Those of us who qualify line up at the table where the HR admin-
istrator hands out the waiver we must sign before the company
will mail out our severance check. A few of us actually take

the time to read it and ask the HR administrator questions. He listens, and then refers us to the legal department. It is our right to ask questions before signing the waiver, he says. He also says doing so will delay the mailing of our check until the legal department makes sure we are satisfied with their answer. We sign. No more questions.

The line for food moves fast. We sit down to eat. Some of us are crying, or go from table to table, shaking hands and hugging. The company has set up a big screen, and pictures of various company events from the past flash before our eyes. The company picnic. Winners of the Halloween costume contest. Mud volleyball. The company softball team. All to the tune of "The Way We Were" playing in the background. The eyes of the security guards stationed at each exit continually sweep over the room.

Some of us are young, still in our twenties. We live with mom and dad, they give us a break on the rent so we can afford the shiny new car we drive. We take classes at the community college. We go clubbing on the weekends. Things don't work out, we can always join the military. We'll be okay.

Some of us have been through this before and never recovered. We filed bankruptcy, cut up the credit cards. Now we live paycheck to paycheck. Eat on the cheap so we can afford cable. We drive used cars from the last decade and live in one-bedroom apartments filled with thrift-store furniture. We buy lottery tickets, regularly. First thing tomorrow morning we'll be on the phone opening a claim for unemployment benefits. It could be worse.

But some of us played the game. Over the years we scratched and crawled into the comfy jobs paying a decent wage. We became Team Leaders and Supervisors. We learned how to smile and swallow at the same time. Feathered our nest with contributions to the 401(k) and company stock purchased with the employee discount plan. Got a mortgage, a second mortgage, kids in college, two (almost new) gas-guzzling SUVs, and a map to retirement in our back pocket.

For them, this is all there is.

I push away from the table, pick up my box of personal belongings, and head for the parking lot. As I approach the exit, Ed, a middle-aged, baldheaded black guy whose broad shoulders and thick arms gives the impression he could have played defensive back on any college football team, calls me over to the security desk. He is a Bears fan who likes to give me a dose of good-humored shit, busting my balls whenever I wear my Raiders t-shirt to work. I'm going to miss him and figure this will be our last chitchat.

"Sorry man," he says. "I have to do this." He looks in my box and rifles through the contents, looking for office supplies. A coveted stapler or a package of precious Post-It Notes.

Then he waves me on.

I sit in the company parking lot for the last time, in my eleven-year-old red Hyundai Elantra. It needs an oil change and new tires, but that will have to wait. I think of the new wave of layoffs reported this morning in the newspaper, a front-page picture of hundreds lined up outside the doors of a new business in town with a dozen new jobs. I start my car and back out, then pull forward to the automated gate. I wait as the motor is activated and the chain pulls the gate on its little wheels until there is enough room for me to drive out into the street. I take one last look in the rearview mirror, watch my ex-coworkers trickle out into the parking lot, each carrying a box under their arm as they walk to their cars and trucks. An old army saying comes to mind: "If you're gonna fuck me, at least give me a kiss." Then my gaze shifts to my own reflection in the mirror. I see what the interviewers will see, a double chin, a graying beard, and crow's feet in the corners of my tired-looking eyes. This is not good.

A honking horn from the car waiting behind me breaks the spell. I drive out into the street.

Two.

During the 1990s, I lived in Rockford, Illinois: one of those small towns that keeps getting listed on the Forbes Magazine list of "lousiest places to live in the U.S." They drink a lot in Rockford. During the winter, the residents form dart leagues and bowling teams so they can meet at a bar and drink. During the summer, they form softball leagues so they can meet after the game and drink. The Rock River splits the town in two. Old houses and most of the black and brown residents on the west side, newer houses and most of the white residents on the east side. Being the hometown of Cheap Trick is Rockford's claim to fame, that and a prominent porn star they don't like to talk about. And yes, places of worship almost match the number of bars and dives, of which there are a multitude.

I was working on the east side for Blevins & Nubbs Booksellers as their Community Relations Manager. I organized the monthly calendar of store events. My duties included contacting authors for appearances and booking local musicians to play in the café. I started poetry workshops and book clubs and cajoled my fellow employees to put on smelly Cat-in-the-Hat or Clifford costumes (passed around from store to store) for story hour in the kids' books department.

Once, out of curiosity, I converted my salary to an hourly rate. It was barely over eight dollars an hour. Sometimes I hocked my VCR twice in the same month, other times my gold ring. Or I'd get a loan from one of those places that gave advances on my next paycheck. I had to eat. I had to buy gas and pay for dry cleaning. I was making $17,500 a year. When I quit the bookstore for a higher-paying job, they paid me for my unused vacation time. A month later, I got a letter from them; vacation pay was issued in error. Could they please have their money back?

I remember the high arc of the wadded-up request for the return of their vacation check, floating through the air, dropping down into the wastebasket across the room with a *whoosh*. Nothing but net. The crowd went wild.

January 1999. My new employer was Konsiko Medical Insurance. The company occupied a couple of buildings downtown. A two-story building with majestic columns and fake Greek architecture, and a tall, multi-storied office building right on the banks of the Rock River. I worked on the third floor in the call center. Rows and rows of desks, phones, computer monitors, keyboards, and headsets. All of us talking at the same time; a cacophony of voices all saying at once, "Hello. Thank you for calling Konsiko Medical Insurance. My name is ____. How may I help you today?" I learned a new language. Co-pay, Deductible, Out of Pocket, Pre-existing Condition, PPO, HMO, Primary Care Provider, In Network, Out of Network, Policy Exclusion.

I learned the art of how to say "no" without actually saying it: Your prescription benefit is maxed out for the year, all your prescriptions will now be "out of pocket" ... the procedure is "excluded" from coverage ... the doctor was "out of network," so you will have a higher "co-pay" ... you did not get a "referral" from your "primary care provider," so the office visit to that specialist is not covered ... your doctor used an "out of network" lab so your "in-network co-pay" does not apply ... your "annual" benefit for chemo has been "depleted" and it won't be covered again until next year ... the address for appeals is....

Sometimes the person on the other end of the line erupted in a burst of anger and name-calling; other times they broke down and cried. I preferred the name-calling.

The Konsiko Medical Insurance company magazine liked to feature articles about the tropical resort reserved for their sales team's elite performers: ringed with white-sand beaches, a turquoise-blue ocean, and a pool with a bar you could swim up to. Beautiful people were seated at the bar, sipping decadent drinks decorated with colorful little paper umbrellas. Everyone was laughing and having a great time with their glowing tans, washboard abs, wet and sexy swimsuits, and perfectly straight white teeth. Contrast this with the call center's morale boosters: "blue jean" Fridays when the dress code was relaxed and we were allowed to wear comfortable clothes for eight hours.

Or the monthly potluck: crock pots of all shapes and sizes lined up in the break room emitting the aroma of cocktail weenies cooking in their "special" sauces, sloppy joe hamburger meat, store-bought buckets of potato and macaroni salads, and one of those huge sheet cakes from the local supermarket covered in a thick sugary frosting that dissolved tooth enamel after three bites.

We were the belly of the beast.

When the company's plan to expand by acquiring the nation's largest mobile home lender backfired, Konsiko's stock went from thirty-five dollars a share to (literally) a handful of pennies. Every day I reported for work was like reliving all the desperation and anxiety of the last hours of the Titanic. They announced they would be laying off a few of us at a time, every month, until we were all gone. I volunteered to be one of the first. Upon receiving my severance check, I rushed to the bank to make sure it was good.

And the CEO who ran the operation into the ground? With the perfect timing of a pilot ejecting from his plane just before the crash, he saved his own ass, his golden parachute landing him gently at poolside, where he promptly found a seat at the bar and ordered a mango-pineapple-banana-passion fruit margarita.

THREE.

I decided to take my measly severance and start over in a new town. Fuck, a new *state*.

Driving into Albuquerque after two and a half days on the road, I thought it strange that every house, garage, apartment, bungalow, tool shed, outhouse, and doghouse was stuccoed *and* had security bars on every window and door, but I wasn't surprised. I watched the reality TV show *Cops* and knew that the show loved visiting Albuquerque. The TV show portrayed a Mecca of meth labs, prostitution, break-ins, and domestic violence. And every episode always featured some mishap involving a man dressed in women's clothes. I was up for a little adventure. I found an apartment my first afternoon in town.

Since I was collecting unemployment, I knew I could take my time looking for work. I soon found out that my new hometown was a magnet for call centers. Cell phone companies, health insurance, AOL, JC Penney, Bank of America, and even Victoria's Secret had their inbound customer service operations in the Duke City. I could take my pick.

I ended up at UnityHealth, another medical insurance company. UnityHealth was bigger and, initially, better than Konsiko. They offered me the most pay. The training took six long weeks. When the trainer ran out of things for us to do, we played trivia games. We had potlucks, celebrated the holidays with a gift exchange and birthdays with cake and ice cream. We became a tight-knit group. We graduated from the training room to staffing phones, where it did not take long to figure out the company's standard operating procedure.

The typical medical insurance company knows it can't get around the little stuff: the office visit because Johnny has the sniffles or little Amber has a sore throat. It's the big stuff they fight tooth and nail. The CT scans, the surgical procedures (big and small), cancer treatments and MRIs, and the expensive tests to determine if the policy holder has a deadly disease that will cost the insurance company an arm and a leg. If a customer came to UnityHealth with something like that, the company required prior authorization. On paper it made sense; the patient gathered all relative records and treatment notes, including a letter by the doctor who prescribed the procedure which made the case for why all this expensive stuff was being deemed necessary. All the paperwork was sent via the only fax number UnityHealth had set up for this process. The customer was told to wait thirty days for a "determination," as a team of highly qualified healthcare professionals (who were also collecting a paycheck from the insurance company) decided in their employer's favor; i.e., some other "cost effective" treatment would have to be implemented first.

When the customer called after the required thirty-day waiting period, there was no record of the documents ever being received. Nowhere. Nada. The caller then proceeded to chew my ear off as I sat quietly imagining a small closet where this mysterious fax machine was buried under a pile of medical records coming in from all over the country, twenty-four hours a day, seven days a week. Sooner or later, the fax machine jammed or ran out of paper. And as far as I could tell, that's it. That's the UnityHealth prior authorization department. Even though I knew where the call was headed, I was not allowed to ask if they wanted to speak to a supervisor. The caller had to explicitly ask for one before I could initiate a transfer. The supervisors always asked "Did the caller request a supervisor?" And they always sighed when I answered in the affirmative.

The last straw was the day my new supervisor followed me to the john to make sure my visit was legit, peeking his head in the door as I stood at the urinal with my dick in my hand. Upon finishing my business, I walked over to his cubicle and handed him a note that simply said,

"I quit." Then I gathered my belongings and walked out the door. I had been employed by them for eight months.

FOUR.

There are rules. Not the ones in the employee handbook, but the ones we learn to follow so we can survive in the workplace. And the day I walked away from UnityHealth I broke the most important one: Never, ever, quit a job unless there is one waiting in the wings. My defiant gesture at UnityHealth felt good ... for about ten minutes. And soon proved to be one of the more boneheaded things I'd ever done. First, I assumed that the job market would be the same one that had offered me three jobs at once when I chose the position at UnityHealth. Second, by voluntarily leaving the job, I had squelched any chance of collecting unemployment.

The first month I lived off some company stock I had cashed in. Panic mode had not set in since I thought a new job was out there, somewhere, waiting for me to apply. I was wrong. Perhaps if I had not stubbornly resolved to get out of the call center industry, I might have been back to work sooner. One month turned into two, then three ...

Funny things happen when you're out of work for five months. I began questioning why I got a worthless degree in

English, instead of something more marketable, like business administration or engineering. Why hadn't I learned a trade? You never hear of a plumber or a mechanic going hungry.

My days blurred into one another. I'd go to bed thinking it was Sunday and wake up on Wednesday. I started staying up until three or four a.m., sleeping until one or two in the afternoon. I found out I had it in me to forego my daily shower and I stopped changing the sheets on my bed. It wasn't like I had someplace to be or people to impress. Wearing my clothes more than once before washing them stretched the money I needed for the laundromat. I had a couple of credit cards, but I was only paying the minimum amount due, which was basically interest. So when I missed my monthly payment, the credit card companies practically doubled the interest rate. Throw in penalties for not paying my bill, and I was seriously expecting a visit by a couple of guys named Vinnie and Rocky. Instead, I got phone calls. Lots of phone calls. Exotic accents, soft spoken and polite. I knew they weren't calling from this country. When I asked for their names they gave "Thomas" or "Heather." When I asked where they were calling from, they evaded the question, steering the conversation back to my unpaid balance. I told them I couldn't find a decent job. This always created a moment of awkward silence on their end, but they recovered as they went back to the script. They wanted to sign me up for automatic payment through my checking account. They wanted to work out a payment plan. I said no thanks and hung up. Rent first, utilities and food second. Those were my priorities. Visa could suck my balls.

Finally realizing how close I was to joining the homeless men and women who walk up and down Central Ave., begging for change, napping on bus stop benches, and shitting in the alleys for lack of public toilets, I answered an ad for insurance claims processors. Red Badge Medical Insurance had contracted a temp agency to provide them with qualified bodies. Going through a temp agency relieved them from being responsible for benefits, payroll, and all the other stuff required when hiring additional workers. The temp agency conducted a five-minute interview, administered a test to establish my keyboard proficiency, and gave me their stamp of approval. The position was paid $9.10 an hour. And once I completed training, Red Badge would hire me full-time and pay me twelve dollars an hour (or more) based on my experience. Konsiko had cross-trained me in claims processing, so I figured I was in. All I had to do now was pass the mandatory piss test.

I've often wondered who determines who takes this "mandatory" test. After I empty my pockets in front of the person administering the test, I am handed a plastic cup with a twist-off lid. I enter the restroom, closing the door behind me. I stand in front of the toilet, my limp penis in my hand and plastic cup in the other, the windows and sink drain are sealed tight, and a stranger waits outside the door to make sure I don't try any funny stuff. I wonder why we don't make our elected officials do the same thing. Or the CEOs who make the greedy decisions that devastate the corporations they lead. Instead, we make the greeters at Walmart and the fry cooks at McDonald's prove their innocence so they can earn a minimum wage.

The trainers at Red Badge were a cozy bunch. They loved talking about social and family life. They spent just as much time shooting the shit with each other as they did training us. I knew that Kathy lived for her weekly trips to the casinos. I foresaw an intervention in her future, complete with family members pleading with her as her little girl sat on her lap crying, "But mommy, you promised I'd go to college." Pedro played the trumpet (on the weekend) and liked to jam with other musicians at some of the local bars and clubs. He talked like a devoted husband and father, but he constantly combed his hair and gave certain women more attention than the rest of the class. I thought he was an asshole. The claims processing was going to be more automated than what I was used to.

This job was more about production and speed. I wasn't really going to have to spend much time using my previous job experience reviewing medical benefits and determining if a claim qualified or not. My fellow trainees were excited about becoming full-fledged employees of the company upon completion of training. Talk of what they thought the starting pay rate would be was always in the air. Twelve dollars an hour seemed to be the consensus, but in their wildest dreams, fifteen dollars an hour seemed plausible. But some of us began to hear things from the training class that had come before us.

They were already on the floor processing claims. During breaks and lunch, I overheard some of them talking amongst themselves. They were a disgruntled group, because they had been processing claims for a month and were still collecting their check from the temp agency. No pay increase, either. Once my training class got word of this, we began asking Pedro and Kathy questions. They hemmed and hawed, proclaiming they had nothing to do with what the temp agency had promised. Things got so bad the company called a special meeting for all the contract workers from the temp agency.

The HR manager stood before us and announced that the company did not have any control over what we had been told beforehand, and that the following should answer any questions we had:

1. Upon completion of training, our pay would go from $9.10 an hour to $9.25.
2. The company didn't have any more full-time positions available, but there was always the possibility jobs would be available in the near future, so we were encouraged to continue as temps and impress the bosses with our attitude, attendance, and productivity.
3. End of story, take it or leave it.

I wasn't surprised, although many of my fellow trainees were visibly upset. The sounds of car doors slamming and tires squealing filled the air as they roared out of the parking lot at the end of the meeting. The next day, two people called in sick. The trend continued through the rest of our training.

The most humiliating experience was the morning we had to attend a companywide pep rally at a local hotel. The company was celebrating their latest quarterly report and handing out meager bonuses to all who qualified. As temp employees, we did not qualify, but we had to sit there and watch people acting like complete idiots, doing asinine company cheers. Screaming like the shameless audience at a TV game show every time a name was called out and the worker jumped on stage to claim their bonus.

After it was all done, all the temp workers were advised that (as a show of appreciation) we had something waiting for us in the back of the conference room. We got up from our seats and lined up in front of a table staffed by an HR rep. I was in the back of the line, so I couldn't see at first what was being handed out. Gift cards for Walmart? Movie passes? I saw one of my coworkers walking out, shaking his head in disbelief.

In his hand was a PayDay candy bar.

acknowledgments

The poet would like to thank the following poetry journals and anthologies for welcoming his work in their publications. (Some poems have been revised for this collection.)

"leaving a tip at the Red Roof Inn," *Big Hammer* #21, Inequity Press/Vendetta Books

"the Pope's poop," *HEARTFIRE: Second Revolutionary Poets Brigade Anthology*, Kallatumba Press

"milagro 11" & "milagro 15," *Trickster, A Literary Journal*, Northern New Mexico College

"current affair," *Chiron Review* #117

"the story of my life" & "the shocking end to the story of my life," *Bombfire*, bombfirelit.com

"Neo teaches me a lesson," *Barrio Panther Literature Magazine*

"how not to have any children and feel no regrets" & "menudo," Silver Birch Press, silverbirchpress.wordpress.com

"13 angels rising," *The Best American Poetry*, blog.bestamericanpoetry.com

"13 angels rising," *As Us*, asusjournal.org

"my bullet," "trickle this" & "60,000 dead," *The Asylum Floor*, theasylumfloor.blogspot.com

"isolation," "smokers" & "leaving a tip at the Red Roof Inn," *Fixed and Free Quarterly*

"sorting and pricing clothes for the local thrift store," *San Pedro River Review*, Spring 2023

"when I was a UPS man," *As It Ought to Be*, asitoughttobemagazine.com

about the author

RICHARD VARGAS WAS BORN in Compton, California. He earned his B.A. at Cal State University, Long Beach, where he studied under Gerald Locklin and Richard Lee. He edited and published five issues of *The Tequila Review* from 1978 to 1980, publishing early works by Jimmy Santiago Baca, Alberto Rios, Nila Northsun, Dennis Cooper, Ron Koertge, and many more. His first book, *McLife*, was featured twice on Garrison Keillor's *Writer's Almanac*. A second book, *American Jesus*, was published by Tia Chucha Press in 2007. His third book, *Guernica, revisited*, was published in 2014 by Press 53 and was featured once more on *The Writer's Almanac*. *How A Civilization Begins* was published by Mouthfeel Press in 2022. Vargas received his MFA from the University of New Mexico in 2010, where he workshopped his poetry with Joy Harjo. He received the 2011 Taos Summer Writers' Conference's Hispanic Writer Award, was on the faculty of the 2012 10th National Latino Writers Conference, and facilitated a workshop at the 2015 Taos Summer Writers' Conference. Vargas edited and published *The Más Tequila Review* from 2009 to 2015, featuring poets from across the country. He has read his poetry to audiences from Los Angeles to Indianapolis and many locales in between. Currently, he resides in Wisconsin, near the lake where Otis Redding's plane crashed.

His work history is long and varied. Some of the jobs he's had since the 1970s: fry and grill cook, women's shoes salesman, bank employee, gas station attendant, retail salesman (paint/men's clothes/auto repair and service,) warehouseman, infantry lieutenant, warehouse supervisor, UPS deliveryman, massage therapist, bookseller, bookstore events coordinator, inbound call center CSR (for several companies). He is now retired.

about the press

CASA URRACA PRESS PUBLISHES creative nonfiction, poetry, and other works by authors and artists we believe in. New Mexico and the U.S. Southwest are rich in creative and literary talent, and the rest of the world deserves to experience our perspectives. So we champion books that belong in the conversation—books with the power, compassion, and variety to bring very different people closer together.

We are proudly centered in the high desert somewhere near Abiquiú, New Mexico. Our books are available through independent booksellers everywhere. You can visit us online at casaurracapress.com for exquisite editions of our books and to register for workshops with our authors.

www.ingramcontent.com/pod-product-compliance
Lightning Source LLC
Chambersburg PA
CBHW031243120626
46545CB00007B/2622